MEAL PREP COOKBOOK

HEALTHY

Get Started with this 28 Day Meal Plans With 44 Quick and Easy Recipes So You Can Savor Nutrient Rich, Delicious and Healthy Homemade Food Regularly.

Table of Contents

INTRODUCTION

A healthy diet is fundamental for acceptable wellbeing and nourishment. It secures you against numerous constant no communicable illnesses, like coronary illness, diabetes and disease. Eating an assortment of food varieties and devouring less salt, sugars and immersed and mechanically delivered trans-fats, are fundamental for healthy diet.

What we eat can influence every one of the cycles in the body, including cell recovery, irritation, assimilation and rest. So it's nothing unexpected that after even just 28 days of eating great you can hope to look better, yet feel a ton better, as well. Healthy meals highlights organic products, vegetables, entire grains, and sans fat or low-fat milk and milk items incorporates an assortment of protein food sources like fish, lean meats and poultry, eggs, vegetables (beans and peas), soy items, nuts, and seeds.

Is low in soaked fats, trans fats, cholesterol, salt (sodium), and added sugars. This book contains such recipes which have part of medical advantages. Inside seven days of eating better, you'll notice that your energy level has gone up. You'll be improving rest and dealing with every one of the exercises of the day like a professional. Odds are, you will not feel very bloated.

1. Roasted Chicken and Vegetables

Total Time: 1 hr. | Prep: 15 min. | Bake: 45 min. |
Makes 6 servings

INGREDIENTS

- 2 pounds red potatoes (around 6 medium), cut into 3/4-inch pieces
- 1 enormous onion, coarsely chopped
- 2 tablespoons olive oil
- 3 garlic cloves, minced
- 1-1/4 teaspoons salt, separated
- 1 teaspoon dried rosemary, squashed, isolated
- 3/4 teaspoon pepper, separated
- 1/2 teaspoon paprika
- 6 bone-in chicken thighs (around 2-1/4 pounds), skin eliminated
- 6 cups new child spinach (around 6 ounces)

DIRECTIONS

1. Preheat oven to 425°. In a huge bowl, consolidate potatoes, onion, oil, garlic, 3/4 teaspoon salt, 1/2 teaspoon rosemary and 1/2 teaspoon pepper; throw to cover. Move to a 15x10x1-in. preparing pan covered with cooking shower.

2. In a small bowl, blend paprika and the leftover salt, rosemary and pepper. Sprinkle chicken with paprika combination; organize over vegetables. Cook until a thermometer embedded in chicken peruses 170°-175° and vegetables are simply delicate, 35-40 minutes.

3. Eliminate chicken to a serving platter; keep warm. Top vegetables with spinach. Broil until vegetables are delicate and spinach is shriveled, 8-10 minutes longer. Mix vegetables to join; present with chicken.

4. Set up your sheet-pan supper the prior night and simply pop it into the preheated oven to prepare. This serves to profoundly enhance the chicken, a shared benefit!

5. In the event that you need a more extravagant dish, use skin-on chicken, and on the off chance that you need a lighter dish, utilize

bone-in chicken breasts. Make certain to cook bone-in breasts just to 165-170 degrees, since more slender meat can get dry at higher temperatures.

2. Ham Steaks with Gruyere, Bacon & Mushrooms

Total Time Prep/Total Time: 25 min. Makes 4 servings

INGREDIENTS

- 2 tablespoons spread
- 1/2 pound cut new mushrooms
- 1 shallot, finely chopped
- 2 garlic cloves, minced
- 1/8 teaspoon coarsely ground pepper
- 1 completely cooked boneless ham steak (around 1 pound), cut into 4 pieces
- 1 cup shredded Gruyere cheddar
- 4 bacon strips, cooked and disintegrated
- 1 tablespoon minced new parsley, optional

DIRECTIONS

1. In an enormous nonstick skillet, heat spread over medium-high heat. Add mushrooms and shallot; cook and mix 4-6 minutes or until delicate. Add garlic and pepper; cook brief longer. Eliminate from pan; keep warm. Wipe skillet clean.

2. In same skillet, cook ham over medium heat 3 minutes. Turn; sprinkle with cheddar and bacon. Cook, covered, 2-4 minutes longer or until cheddar is softened and ham is heated through. Present with mushroom blend. Whenever wanted, sprinkle with parsley.

3.   Lemony Parsley Baked Cod

Total Time Prep/Total Time: 25 min. Makes 4

servings

INGREDIENTS

- 3 tablespoons minced fresh parsley
- 2 tablespoons lemon juice
- 1 tablespoon grated lemon zest
- 1 tablespoon olive oil
- 2 garlic cloves, minced
- 1/4 teaspoon salt
- 1/8 teaspoon pepper
- 4 cod fillets (6 ounces each)
- 2 green onions, chopped

DIRECTIONS

1. Preheat oven to 400°. In a small bowl, mix the first seven INGREDIENTS. Place cod in an ungreased 11x7-in. baking dish; top with parsley mixture. Drizzle with green onions. Bake, covered, 10-15 minutes or until fish flakes easily with a fork.

4.   Easy Firehouse Chili

Total Time Prep: 20 min. Cook: 1-1/2 hours Makes 16 servings (4 quarts)

INGREDIENTS

- 2 tablespoons canola oil
- 4 pounds lean ground hamburger (90% lean)
- 2 medium onions, chopped
- 1 medium green pepper, chopped
- 4 jars (16 ounces every) kidney beans, washed and depleted
- 3 jars (28 ounces each) stewed tomatoes, cut up
- 1 can (14-1/2 ounces) hamburger stock
- 3 tablespoons bean stew powder
- 2 tablespoons ground coriander
- 2 tablespoons ground cumin

- 4 garlic cloves, minced
- 1 teaspoon dried oregano

DIRECTIONS

1. In a Dutch oven, heat canola oil over medium heat. Brown hamburger in clumps, disintegrating meat, until not, at this point pink; channel and put in a safe spot. Add onions and green pepper; cook until delicate. Return meat to Dutch oven. Mix in excess INGREDIENTS. Heat to the point of boiling. Diminish heat; stew, covered, until flavors are mixed, around 1-1/2 hours.

2. Canola oil is high in monounsaturated fat, a sort that assists with diminishing blood cholesterol levels, and low in immersed fat, which can build blood cholesterol. Olive oil would likewise taste extraordinary in this formula and has similar solid fat properties.

3. Lean ground turkey (93% lean) contains 53% less fat and 38% less soaked fat than ordinary ground turkey (85% lean). It works extraordinary in goulashes, tacos and different dishes that utilization disintegrated meat.

Higher-fat meat turns out better for burgers or meatloaf.

5. Chicken Tequila Fettuccine

INGREDIENTS

- 1-2 pounds dry spinach fettuccine (or 2 pounds fresh)
- 1/2 cup chopped cilantro (2 tablespoons for garnish/finishing)
- 2-tablespoons of chopped fresh garlic
- 2-tablespoons chopped jalapeno pepper (seeds and veins can be removed if a milder flavor is desired)
- 3-tablespoons unsalted butter (reserve tablespoons per container)
- 1/2 cup of chicken stock
- 2-tablespoons of tequila

- 2-tablespoons of freshly squeezed lime juice
- 3-tablespoons of soy sauce
- 1/2 pound chicken breast diced 3/4 inch
- 1/4 cup red onion thinly sliced
- 1 1/2 cup of red bell pepper thinly sliced
- 1/2 cup of yellow bell pepper thinly sliced
- 1/2 cup green pepper thinly sliced
- 1 1/2 cups of cream

DIRECTIONS

1. Quickly prepare to boil salted water for cooking pasta; cook dinner al dente, for dry pasta for 8 to 10 minutes, for bubbly for about three minutes. Pasta can be cooked, rinsed, and oiled slightly ahead of time, after which it is "flashed" in boiling water or cooked to match the sauce/topping.

2. Mix 1/3 cup of cilantro, garlic, and jalapeno over medium heat in 2 tablespoons of oil for four to 5 minutes. Remove lime juice, tequila, and stock. Bring the combination to a boil and cook to a pasty consistency until reduced; put aside.

3. Pour over the diced soy sauce; Set aside for 5 minutes. Meanwhile, prepare evening onions and peppers with the last of butter over medium heat, stirring occasionally. Toss and add the reserved vegetables and cream when the vegetable wilt (go limp), add the chook and soy sauce.

4. Bring the sauce to a boil; cook gently until the chicken has melted and the sauce is thick (about 3 minutes).

6. Salmon-and-Rice Soup

Prep time: 20 min Serving 4

INGREDIENTS

- 3/4 c. long-grain rice
- 1/2 lb. salmon filet
- 2 tbsp. soy sauce
- 1 tbsp. Asian sesame oil
- 10 cilantro stems
- 1/2 tbsp. minced new ginger
- 1 tsp. salt
- 2 c. canned low-sodium chicken stock or natively constructed stock
- 4 c. water
- 3 scallions including green tops

- This fixing shopping module is made and kept up by an outsider, and imported onto this page. You might have the option to discover more data about this and comparative substance on their site.

DIRECTIONS

1. Heat a medium pot of salted water to the point of boiling. Mix in the rice and bubble until practically delicate, around 10 minutes. Channel.
2. Coat the salmon with the soy sauce and sesame oil.
3. In an enormous pot, join the cooked rice, the cilantro stems, the ginger, salt, stock and water. Heat to the point of boiling. Decrease the heat and stew, covered, blending at times, for 15 minutes.
4. Add the salmon to the pot. Stew, covered, until the salmon is simply done, around 5 minutes. Eliminate the cilantro stems. Serve the soup decorated with the cilantro leaves and scallions.

5. Notes: We utilized long-grain rice for our soup. In China and Japan, it would be made with short-grain, which is starchier and disintegrates into the soup all the more promptly. On the off chance that you need to go the short-grain course, arborio is promptly accessible.

6. Wine Recommendation: Pairing this soup with wine might be somewhat of a stretch. An ale lager is a vastly improved decision. Most awesome aspect all: little jars of warm, tart purpose.

7. Easy Spaghetti Carbonara

INGREDIENTS

- 1/4 cup of flour
- 1/4 cup of butter
- 1 liter of milk
- 1/8 teaspoon of pepper
- 1/2 teaspoon of salt
- 18 oz. bacon sliced extra thick
- 1/4 cup of olive oil
- 12 oz. sliced mushrooms
- 6-tablespoons of chopped shallots
- Cook 1-pound of spaghetti according to the package insert
- 2-teaspoons finely chopped parsley
- 1/2 cup of grated Parmesan cheese

- 2-ounces of freshly grated Fontina cheese

DIRECTIONS

1. Melt butter over medium heat in a 4-quart casserole.

2. Remove the meal and prepare dinner for 1 minute. Add milk, pepper, and pepper, and start with a wire beater until the mixture boils slightly. Reduce the heat and cook for 5 minutes, even if the sauce thickens. Stir the Fontina cheese into the sauce and let it soften in the sauce. Stay warm.

3. Prepare the bacon thoroughly for dinner. Drain on paper towels. Cut into 1/4-inch pieces and whisk in the sauce. In a large skillet, soften the olive oil over medium heat. Attach sliced onions and chopped mushrooms and fry until golden brown; adhere to the sauce. Cook spaghetti in the direction of the box. Drain well and add the parsley to the sauce. Mix well and move to a serving table. Sprinkle with Parmesan cheese and let it function as quickly as possible.

8.   Oriental Apple Bee Salad

Prep time 10 min serves: 2

INGREDIENTS

- 1 lb. skinless chicken breast 2-servings
- 2-tablespoons of olive oil
- 1/2 teaspoon of salt
- 1/4 teaspoon black pepper
- 1/2 cup of sliced almonds
- 8-cups of romaine lettuce
- 1/4 cup sliced carrots
- 1/2 cup of crispy rice noodles
- 4-tablespoons Applebee's Oriental Salad Dressing

DIRECTIONS

1. Heat the grill to medium, or heat a sturdy iron skillet or grill pan over medium heat. Place the hand between two 'plastic wrap' and lift them to 3/8 min. Fizzy with the other oil and top with some pepper and pepper.

2. Grill them for 5 to 7 minutes on each side, until cooked through. Place them on a plate for four to five minutes rather than sliced to relax.

3. Roast the almonds in a little dry sauce over the heat of it

4. Supervise them - there is a high-quality line between toasted almonds and burnt almonds! Shake the pan gently when you start to smell the almonds, toast for a few more seconds, and immediately put the almonds on a paper towel. Let them cool down or.

5. Like salads, by putting down the lettuce first, 3 to 4 choices start with the food.

6. Sprinkle each with 2-tablespoons of carrots, 1/4 cup of crispy rice noodles, and 1/4 cup of toasted almonds. Place the poultry on top. Serve with loads of the Applebee's Oriental Salad Dressing.

9. Chorizo & Grits Breakfast Bowls

Total Time Prep/Total Time: 30 min. Makes 6 servings

INGREDIENTS

- 2 teaspoons olive oil
- 1 bundle (12 ounces) completely cooked chorizo chicken frankfurters or kind of decision, cut
- 1 enormous zucchini, chopped
- 3 cups water
- 3/4 cup speedy cooking corn meal
- 1 can (15 ounces) dark beans, flushed and depleted
- 1/2 cup shredded cheddar

- 6 enormous eggs
- Optional: Pico de Gallo and chopped new cilantro

DIRECTIONS

1. In an enormous skillet, heat oil over medium heat. Add hotdog; cook and mix until delicately browned, 2-3 minutes. Add zucchini; cook and mix until delicate, 4-5 minutes longer. Eliminate from pan; keep warm.

2. Then, in an enormous saucepan, heat water to the point of boiling. Gradually mix in corn meal. Decrease heat to medium-low; cook, covered, until thickened, blending occasionally, around 5 minutes. Mix in beans and cheddar until mixed. Eliminate from heat.

3. Wipe skillet clean; cover with cooking shower and spot over medium heat. In clusters, break 1 egg at an at once. Promptly lessen heat to low; cook until whites are totally set and yolks start to thicken yet are not hard, around 5 minutes.

4. To serve, partition corn meal blend among 6 dishes. Top with chorizo combination, eggs and, whenever wanted, Pico de Gallo and cilantro.

10. Simple Poached Salmon

Total Time Prep: 10 min. Cook: 1-1/2 hours Makes 4 servings

INGREDIENTS

- 2 cups water
- 1 cup white wine
- 1 medium onion, sliced
- 1 celery rib, slashed
- 1 medium carrot, sliced
- 2 tablespoons lemon juice
- 3 thyme sprigs
- 1 fresh rosemary sprig
- 1 bay leaf
- 1/2 teaspoon salt
- 1/4 teaspoon pepper

- 4 salmon fillets (1-1/4 inches thick and 6 ounces each)
- Lemon wedges

DIRECTIONS

1. Firstly In a 3-qt. slow cooker combines the first 11 INGREDIENTS. Cook, covered, on low 45 minutes.
2. Carefully place fillets in liquid; add additional warm water (120° to 130°) to cover if needed. Cook, covered, just until fish flakes easily with a fork (a thermometer inserted in fish should read at least 145°), 45-55 minutes. Then Remove fish from cooking liquid. And Serve warm or cold with lemon wedges.

11. Apple Balsamic Chicken

Total Time Prep: 15 min. Cook: 4 hours Makes 4 servings

INGREDIENTS

- 4 bone-in chicken thighs (around 1-1/2 pounds), skin eliminated
- 1/2 cup chicken stock
- 1/4 cup apple juice or juice
- 1/4 cup balsamic vinegar
- 2 tablespoons lemon juice
- 1/2 teaspoon salt
- 1/2 teaspoon garlic powder
- 1/2 teaspoon dried thyme
- 1/2 teaspoon paprika
- 1/2 teaspoon pepper
- 2 tablespoons spread

- 2 tablespoons generally useful flour

DIRECTIONS

1. Spot chicken in a 1-1/2-qt. slow cooker. In a little bowl, consolidate the stock, juice, vinegar, lemon juice and flavors; pour over meat. Cover and cook on low for 4-5 hours or until chicken is delicate.

2. Eliminate chicken; keep warm. Skim fat from cooking fluid. In a little pot, liquefy margarine; mix in flour until smooth. Steadily add cooking fluid. Heat to the point of boiling; cook and mix for 2-3 minutes or until thickened. Present with chicken.

12. Sausage-Stuffed Flank Steak

Total Time Prep: 35 min. Cook: 6 hours Makes 2 servings

INGREDIENTS

- 1/4 cup dried cherries
- 3/4 cup dry red wine or meat stock, separated
- 1 meat flank steak (1-1/2 pounds)
- 3/4 teaspoon salt, separated
- 1/2 teaspoon pepper, separated
- 1 medium onion, finely chopped
- 3 tablespoons olive oil, partitioned
- 4 garlic cloves, minced
- 1/2 cup prepared bread pieces
- 1/4 cup pitted Greek olives, split
- 1/4 cup ground Parmesan cheddar

- 1/4 cup minced new basil
- 1/2 pound mass hot Italian hotdog
- 1 container (24 ounces) marinara sauce
- Hot cooked pasta

DIRECTIONS

1. In a little bowl, join cherries and 1/4 cup wine; let stand 10 minutes. In the mean time, cut steak into four serving-size pieces; level to 1/4-in. thickness. Sprinkle the two sides with 1/2 teaspoon salt and 1/4 teaspoon pepper.

2. In a huge skillet, sauté onion in 1 tablespoon oil until delicate. Add garlic; cook brief longer. Move to an enormous bowl; mix in bread scraps, olives, cheddar, basil, cherry blend and staying salt and pepper. Disintegrate frankfurter over combination and blend well.

3. Spread 1/2 cup hotdog combination over every steak piece. Move up jam move style, beginning with a long side; attach with kitchen string.

4. In a similar skillet, earthy colored meat in leftover oil on all sides. Move to a lubed 3-qt. slow cooker. Top with marinara sauce and

remaining wine. Cook and cook on low for 6-8 hours or until meat is delicate. Present with pasta.

13. Pork with Peach Picante Sauce

Total Time Prep: 20 min. + chilling Cook: 5-1/2 hours Makes 4 servings

INGREDIENTS

- 2 pounds boneless country-style pork ribs
- 2 tablespoons taco seasoning
- 1/2 cup mild salsa
- 1/4 cup peach preserves
- 1/4 cup barbecue sauce
- 2 cups chopped fresh peeled peaches sour sliced peaches, thawed and chopped

DIRECTIONS

1. Firstly In a large bowl tosses ribs with taco seasoning. Cover and refrigerate overnight.

2. Place pork in a 3-qt. slow cooker. In a little bowl, combine the salsa, preserves and barbecue sauce. Pour over ribs. Then Cover and cook on low for 5-6 hours or until meat is tender.

3. Add peaches; cover and cook 30 minutes longer or until peaches are tender.

14. Chicken & Vegetables with Mustard-Herb Sauce

Total Time Prep: 20 min. Cook: 6 hours Makes 4 servings

INGREDIENTS

- 4 medium red potatoes, quartered
- 3 medium parsnips, cut into 1-inch pieces
- 2 medium leeks (white portion only), thinly slashed
- 3/4 cup fresh baby carrots
- 4 chicken leg quarters, skin removed
- 1 can (10-3/4 ounces) condensed cream of chicken soup with herbs, undiluted
- 2 tablespoons minced fresh parsley
- 1 tablespoon new dill or 1 teaspoon dill weed
- 1 tablespoon mustard

DIRECTIONS

1. Then In a 5- or 6-qt. slow cooker, place the potatoes, parsnips, leeks, carrots and chicken; pour soup over top. Cover and cook on low for 6-8 hours or until chicken is tender.

2. Then Remove chicken and vegetables; cover it and keep warm. Stir the parsley, dill and mustard into cooking juices; present with chicken and vegetables.

15. Peppery Chicken with Potatoes

Total Time Prep: 20 min. Cook: 5 hours + standing

Makes 4 servings

INGREDIENTS

- 1 pound red potatoes (around 6 medium), cut into wedges
- 1 huge onion, chopped
- 2 teaspoons salt
- 1 teaspoon paprika
- 1/2 teaspoon onion powder
- 1/2 teaspoon garlic powder
- 1/2 teaspoon dried thyme
- 1/2 teaspoon white pepper
- 1/2 teaspoon cayenne pepper
- 1/4 teaspoon pepper
- 1 oven/fryer chicken (3-1/2 to 4 pounds)

DIRECTIONS

1. Spot potatoes and onion in a 6-qt. slow cooker. In a little bowl, blend flavors. Fold wings under chicken; integrate drumsticks. Rub preparing combination over outside and within chicken. Spot chicken over vegetables.

2. Cook, covered, on low 5-6 hours or until a thermometer embedded in thickest piece of thigh peruses 170°-175°. Eliminate chicken from slow cooker; tent with foil. Let stand 15 minutes prior to cutting.

3. Move vegetables to a platter; keep warm. Whenever wanted, skim fat and thicken cooking juices for sauce. Present with chicken.

16. Chicken Tagine with Pumpkin

Total Time Prep: 35 min. Cook: 5 hours Makes 4 servings

INGREDIENTS

- 1 pound boneless skinless chicken thighs, cut into 1/2-inch pieces
- 1 can (15 ounces) garbanzo beans or chickpeas, flushed and depleted
- 1 can (14-1/2 ounces) diced tomatoes, undrained
- 1 medium green pepper, chopped
- 1 cup canned pumpkin
- 1/4 cup brilliant raisins
- 1 tablespoon maple syrup
- 2 teaspoons ground cumin
- 1 teaspoon ground cinnamon

- 1/2 teaspoon salt
- 1/2 teaspoon ground coriander
- 1/4 teaspoon cayenne pepper
- 1/4 teaspoon ground cloves
- 1/4 teaspoon ground allspice
- 1 tablespoon olive oil
- 1 medium onion, chopped
- 2 garlic cloves, minced
- 1 teaspoon minced new gingerroot
- Hot cooked couscous and chopped new cilantro

DIRECTIONS

1. In a 3-or 4-qt. slow cooker, join the initial 14 INGREDIENTS. In a little skillet, heat oil over medium heat. Add onion; cook and mix until delicate, 5-7 minutes. Add garlic and ginger; cook brief longer. Mix into slow cooker.

2. Cook, covered, on low until chicken is cooked through and vegetables are delicate, 5-6 hours. Present with couscous; sprinkle with cilantro.

17. Mexican Beef-Stuffed Peppers

Total Time Prep: 15 min. Cook: 5 hours Makes 4 servings

INGREDIENTS

- 4 medium green or sweet red peppers
- 1 pound ground hamburger
- 1 bundle (8.8 ounces) prepared to-serve Spanish rice
- 2 cups destroyed Colby-Monterey Jack cheddar, isolated
- 1-1/2 cups salsa
- 1 tablespoon hot pepper sauce
- 1 cup water
- 2 tablespoons minced new cilantro

DIRECTIONS

1. Cut tops off peppers and eliminate seeds; put in a safe spot. In an enormous skillet, cook meat over medium heat until not, at this point pink; channel.

2. Mix in the rice, 1-1/2 cups cheddar, salsa and pepper sauce. Spoon into peppers. Move to a 5-qt. slow cooker. Pour water around peppers.

3. Cover and cook on low for 5-6 hours or until peppers are delicate and filling is heated through. Top with residual cheddar; sprinkle with cilantro.

18. Easy Lamb kleftiko

5 Hours + Marinating Serves 4

INGREDIENTS

- lemon 1 enormous, squeezed
- extra-virgin olive oil 100ml
- dry white wine 175ml
- Dark peppercorns squashed to make ½ tsp.
- garlic 4 cloves, stripped and left entirety
- Dried oregano 2 tsp.
- Ground cumin 1 tsp.
- sheep shanks 4
- Ocean salt drops 1 tsp.
- ready tomato 1 enormous, cut into quarters
- cinnamon stick 1
- waxy potatoes 750g, stripped and cut into reduced down 3D squares
- level leaf parsley a modest bunch, generally chopped

DIRECTIONS:

1. Put the lemon juice, 2 tbsp. oil, wine, pepper, garlic, oregano and cumin into a blender and whizz. Put the shanks into a bowl, pour over the marinade and back rub well to cover. Cover and chill for at any rate 1 hour yet ideally overnight.

2. Heat the slow cooker to high or low, contingent upon wanted cooking time.

3. Put the meat, marinade, salt, tomato and cinnamon stick into the slow cooker. Cover with the top and cook for 3-4 hours on high, or 6-8 hours on low until totally delicate.

4. At the point when the sheep is cooked through and totally delicate, earthy colored the potatoes in 3 tbsp. of olive oil in a griddle over a medium-high heat until they start to shading and relax.

5. Eliminate the sheep from the slow cooker, put on a plate and cover firmly with foil.

6. Add the seared potatoes to the slow cooker and blend well. Cover and keep cooking for an additional 45 minutes-1 hour or until the potatoes are cooked and delicate. Add the sheep back to the slow cooker to heat through

again. Check the flavoring, adding more if vital.

7. Present with hard bread and a green serving of mixed greens.

19. Delicious Chicken Curry

Total Time Prep: 20 min. Cook: 4-1/2 hours Makes 4 servings

INGREDIENTS

- 4 bone-in chicken bosom parts, skin eliminated (8 ounces each)
- 1 can (15 ounces) cannellini beans, flushed and depleted
- 3/4 cup meagerly cut sweet onion
- 1/2 cup chopped sweet red pepper
- 1 cup peach salsa
- 1 tablespoon curry powder
- 1/2 teaspoon salt
- 1/4 teaspoon pepper
- 1 cup new green beans, managed and cut down the middle

- 2 tablespoons cornstarch
- 1/2 cup cold water
- 1-1/2 cups chicken stock
- 1-1/2 cups uncooked moment rice

DIRECTIONS

1. Spot the chicken, cannellini beans, onion and red pepper in 4-qt. slow cooker. In a little bowl, join the salsa, curry powder, salt and pepper; pour up and over.

2. Cover and cook on low for 4-5 hours or until chicken is delicate. Mix in green beans. Join cornstarch and water until smooth; continuously mix into slow cooker. Cover and cook on high for 30 minutes or until sauce is thickened.

3. In an huge pot, heat stock to the point of boiling; mix in rice. Cover and eliminate from the heat. Let represent 5 minutes or until fluid is consumed and rice is delicate. Cushion with a fork. Present with chicken and sauce.

20. Waffle Monte Cristos

Total Time Prep/Total Time: 20 min. Makes 4

servings

INGREDIENTS

- 1/2 cup apricot jam
- 8 frozen waffles
- 4 cuts store turkey
- 4 cuts shop ham
- 4 cuts Havarti cheddar (around 3 ounces)
- 4 bacon strips, cooked
- 2 tablespoons margarine, relaxed
- Maple syrup

DIRECTIONS

1. Preheat frying pan over medium heat. Spread jelly more than four waffles. Layer with turkey, ham, cheddar and bacon; top with outstanding waffles. Softly spread exterior of waffles with margarine.

2. Spot on frying pan; cook 4-5 minutes on each side or until brilliant brown and heated through. Present with syrup for plunging.

3. Wellbeing Tip: Yep, this is one debauched sandwich. Use cooking splash rather than spread and cut the bacon and cheddar down the middle to save 130 calories, 7 g immersed fat and very nearly 300 mg sodium for every serving.

21. Spicy Mongolian Beef Salad

Total Time Prep/Total Time: 30 min. Makes 4 servings

INGREDIENTS

- 1/4 cup olive oil
- 2 tablespoons rice vinegar
- 1 tablespoon reduced-sodium soy sauce
- 1 tablespoon sesame oil
- 2 teaspoons minced fresh gingerroot
- 1 small garlic clove, minced
- 1 teaspoon sugar
- BEEF:
- 1 tablespoon reduced-sodium soy sauce
- 2 garlic cloves, minced

- 2 teaspoons sugar
- 1 to 2 teaspoons crushed red pepper flakes
- 1 teaspoon sesame oil
- 1 beef top sirloin steak (1 pound), cut into 1/4-inch strips
- 1 tablespoon olive oil
- SALAD:
- 8 cups torn mixed salad greens
- 1 cup shredded carrots
- 1/2 cup thinly sliced cucumber
- 4 radishes, thinly sliced

DIRECTIONS

1. Whisk together first 7 INGREDIENTS.
2. Combine first 5 beef INGREDIENTS; toss with beef strips. In a large cast-iron or other heavy skillet, heat olive oil over medium-high heat; stir-fry beef mixture until browned, 2-3 minutes. Remove from pan.
3. Combine salad INGREDIENTS; divide among 4 plates. Top with beef. Drizzle with dressing.

22. Spinach-Artichoke Rigatoni

Total Time Prep/Total Time: 30 min. Makes 4 servings

INGREDIENTS

- 3 cups uncooked rigatoni or huge tube pasta
- 1 bundle (10 ounces) frozen creamed spinach
- 1 can (14 ounces) water-stuffed artichoke hearts, washed, depleted and quartered
- 2 cups shredded part-skim mozzarella cheddar, isolated
- 1/4 cup ground Parmesan cheddar
- 1/2 teaspoon salt
- 1/4 teaspoon pepper

DIRECTIONS

1. Preheat grill. Get ready rigatoni and spinach as per bundle DIRECTIONS.

2. Channel pasta, saving 1/2 cup pasta water; get back to pan. Add artichoke hearts, 1/2 cup mozzarella cheddar, Parmesan cheddar, salt, pepper and creamed spinach; throw to join, adding a portion of the held pasta water to thin, whenever wanted.

3. Move to a lubed 2-qt. grill safe preparing dish; sprinkle with residual mozzarella cheddar. Sear 4-6 in. from heat 2-3 minutes or until cheddar is dissolved.

23. Easy Stuffed Peppers recipe

Total Time Prep: 15 min. Cook: 3 hours Makes 4 servings

INGREDIENTS:

- 1/2 cup frozen corn
- 1/3 cup uncooked converted long grain rice
- 1-1/4 teaspoons chili powder
- 1/2 teaspoon ground cumin
- Reduced-fat sour cream, optional
- 4 medium sweet red peppers
- 1 can (15 ounces) black beans, rinsed and drained
- 1 cup shredded pepper jack cheese
- 3/4 cup salsa
- 1 small onion, chopped

DIRECTIONS

1. Firstly cut and discard tops from peppers; remove seeds. In a large bowl, mix beans, cheese, salsa, onion, corn, rice, chili powder and cumin; spoon into peppers. Place in a 5-qt. slow cooker coated with cooking spray.

2. Then Cook, covered, on low until peppers are tender and filling is heated through, 3-4 hours. If desired, serve with sour cream.

24. Tangy Pulled Pork Sandwiches

Total Time Prep: 10 min. Cook: 4 hours Makes 4 servings

INGREDIENTS

- 1 pork tenderloin (1 pound)
- 1 cup ketchup
- 2 tablespoons plus 1-1/2 teaspoons brown sugar
- 2 tablespoons plus 1-1/2 teaspoons cider vinegar
- 1 tablespoon plus 1-1/2 teaspoons Worcestershire sauce
- 1 tablespoon spicy brown mustard
- 1/4 teaspoon pepper
- 4 rolls or buns, split and toasted
- Coleslaw, optional

DIRECTIONS

1. Firstly Cut the tenderloin in half; place in a 3-qt. slow cooker. Combine the ketchup, brown sugar, vinegar, Worcestershire sauce, mustard and pepper; pour over pork.

2. Then Cover and cook on low for 4-5 hours or until meat is tender. Remove meat; shred with 2 forks. Now return to slow cooker; heat through. Serve on toasted rolls or buns, with coleslaw if desired.

25. Easy Ribs Dinner

Total Time Prep: 10 min. Cook: 6-1/4 hours Makes 4 servings

INGREDIENTS

- 2 pounds boneless country-style pork ribs
- 1/2 teaspoon salt
- 1/4 teaspoon pepper
- 8 small red potatoes (about 1 pound), halved
- 4 medium carrots, cut into 1-inch pieces
- 3 celery ribs, cut into 1/2-inch pieces
- 1 medium onion, coarsely chopped
- 3/4 cup water
- 1 garlic clove, crushed
- 1 can (10-3/4 ounces) condensed cream mushroom soup, undiluted

DIRECTIONS

1. Firstly Sprinkle ribs with salt and pepper; transfer to a 4-qt. slow cooker. Add potatoes, carrots, celery, onion, water and garlic. Cook, covered, on low until meat and vegetables are tender, 6-8 hours.

2. Then Remove meat and vegetables; skim fat from cooking juices. Whisk soup into cooking juices; return meat and vegetables to slow cooker. Cook, covered until heated through, 15-30 minutes longer.

26. Creamy Italian Chicken

Total Time Prep: 15 min. Cook: 4 hours Makes 4

servings

INGREDIENTS

- 4 boneless skinless chicken breast parts (6 ounces each)
- 1 envelope Italian plate of mixed greens dressing blend
- 1/4 cup water
- 1 bundle (8 ounces) cream cheddar, mollified
- 1 can (10-3/4 ounces) consolidated cream of chicken soup, undiluted
- 1 can (4 ounces) mushroom stems and pieces, depleted
- Hot cooked pasta or rice
- Minced new oregano, discretionary

DIRECTIONS

1. Spot the chicken in a 3-qt. slow cooker. Consolidate serving of mixed greens dressing blend and water; pour over chicken. Cover and cook on low for 3 hours. Eliminate chicken. Cool marginally; shred meat with two forks. Get back to slow cooker.

2. In a little bowl, beat cream cheddar and soup until mixed. Mix in mushrooms. Pour over chicken. Cover and cook until chicken is delicate, 1 hour longer. Present with pasta or rice. Whenever wanted, sprinkle with oregano.

27. Easy Chutney-Glazed Carrots

Total Time Prep: 15 min. Cook: 4 hours Makes 4 servings

INGREDIENTS

- 1/3 cup mango chutney
- 2 tablespoons sugar
- 2 tablespoons minced new parsley
- 2 tablespoons white wine or unsweetened squeezed apple
- 1 tablespoon Dijon mustard
- 1 tablespoon spread, liquefied
- 1 garlic clove, minced
- 1/2 teaspoon salt
- 1/4 teaspoon ground ginger
- 1/4 teaspoon pepper

- 1 pound new carrots, cut into 1/4-inch cuts (around 4 cups)

DIRECTIONS

1. Spot the initial 10 INGREDIENTS in a 3-qt. slow cooker. Add carrots; throw to join.
2. Cook, covered, on low 4-5 hours or until carrots are delicate. Mix prior to serving.

28. Simmered Turkey Enchiladas

Total Time Prep: 10 min. Cook: 6 hours Makes 4 servings

INGREDIENTS

- 2 pounds turkey thighs or drumsticks
- 1 can (8 ounces) pureed tomatoes
- 1 can (4 ounces) slashed green chilies
- 1/3 cup slashed onion
- 2 tablespoons Worcestershire sauce
- 1 to 2 tablespoons bean stew powder
- 1/4 teaspoon garlic powder
- 8 flour tortillas (6 inches), warmed
- Discretionary fixings: Chopped green onions, cut ready olives, slashed tomatoes, destroyed cheddar, harsh cream and destroyed lettuce

DIRECTIONS

1. Eliminate skin from turkey; place turkey in a 5-qt. slow cooker. In a little bowl, consolidate the pureed tomatoes, chilies, onion, Worcestershire sauce, bean stew powder and garlic powder; pour over turkey. Cover and cook on low until turkey is delicate, 6-8 hours.

2. Eliminate turkey; shred meat with a fork and get back to the slow cooker. Heat through.

3. Spoon around 1/2 cup turkey combination down the focal point of every tortilla. Overlay lower part of tortilla over topping and move off. Add fixings of your decision.

4. Freeze choice: Individually wrap cooled burritos in paper towels and foil; freeze in a cooler compartment. To utilize, eliminate foil; place paper towel-wrapped burrito on a microwave-safe plate. Microwave on high until heated through, 3-4 minutes, turning once. Let stand 20 seconds.

29. Easy Home-Style Chicken Soup

Total Time Prep: 15 min. Cook: 6-1/4 hours Makes 4 servings

INGREDIENTS

- 1 can (14-1/2 ounces) reduced-sodium chicken broth
- 1 can (14-1/2 ounces) diced tomatoes, undrained
- 1 cup cubed cooked chicken
- 1 can (8 ounces) mushroom stems and pieces, drained
- 1/4 cup sliced fresh carrot
- 1/4 cup sliced celery
- 1 bay leaf
- 1/8 teaspoon dried thyme
- 3/4 cup uncooked egg noodles

DIRECTIONS

1. In a 1-1/2-qt. slow cooker, combine the first eight INGREDIENTS. Cover and cook on low for 6 hours. Stir in noodles; cover and cook on high for 15-20 minutes or until tender. Discard bay leaf.

30. Slow & Easy Baby Back Ribs

Total Time Prep: 20 min. Cook: 5 hours Makes 4 servings

INGREDIENTS

- 4 pounds pork infant back ribs, cut into 2-rib partitions
- 1 medium onion, cleaved
- 1/2 cup ketchup
- 1/4 cup pressed brown sugar
- 1/4 cup juice vinegar
- 1/4 cup tomato paste or pureed tomatoes
- 2 tablespoons paprika
- 2 tablespoons Worcestershire sauce
- 1 tablespoon arranged mustard
- 1 teaspoon salt
- 1/4 teaspoon pepper

- 2 tablespoons cornstarch
- 2 tablespoons cold water

DIRECTIONS

1. Spot ribs in a 5-qt. slow cooker. In a little bowl, join the onion, ketchup, earthy colored sugar, vinegar, tomato paste, paprika, Worcestershire, mustard, salt and pepper; pour over ribs. Cover and cook on low for 5-6 hours or until meat is delicate.

2. Eliminate ribs to a serving platter; keep warm. Skim fat from cooking juices; move juices to a little pot. Heat to the point of boiling.

3. Consolidate cornstarch and water until smooth. Step by step mix into the skillet. Heat to the point of boiling; cook and mix for 2 minutes or until thickened. Present with ribs.

31. Tropical Pork Chops

Total Time Prep: 15 min. Cook: 3 hours Makes 4 servings

INGREDIENTS

- 2 containers (23-1/2 ounces each) blended tropical natural product, depleted and slashed
- 3/4 cup defrosted limeade concentrate
- 1/4 cup sweet bean stew sauce
- 1 garlic clove, minced
- 1 teaspoon minced new gingerroot
- 4 bone-in pork flank cleaves (3/4 inch thick and 5 ounces each)
- 1 green onion, finely slashed
- 2 tablespoons minced new cilantro
- 2 tablespoons minced new mint
- 2 tablespoons fragmented almonds, toasted

- 2 tablespoons finely slashed solidified ginger, discretionary
- 1/2 teaspoon ground lime zing

DIRECTIONS

1. In a 3-qt. slow cooker, join the initial 5 INGREDIENTS. Add pork, masterminding cleaves to sit cozily in organic product blend. Cook, covered, on low until meat is delicate (a thermometer embedded in pork should peruse at any rate 145°), 3-4 hours.

2. In a little bowl, blend remaining INGREDIENTS. To serve, eliminate pork cleaves from slow cooker. Using an opened spoon, serve organic product over pork. Sprinkle with spice blend.

32. Sweet Onion & Cherry Pork Chops

Total Time Prep: 15 min. Cook: 3 hours Makes 2 servings

INGREDIENTS

- 1/2 cup fresh or frozen pitted tart cherries, thawed
- 2 tablespoons chopped sweet onion
- 1 tablespoon honey
- 1/2 teaspoon seasoned salt
- 1/4 teaspoon pepper
- 2 boneless pork loin chops (5 ounces each)
- 1 teaspoon cornstarch
- 1 teaspoon cold water

DIRECTIONS

1. Firstly In a 1-1/2-qt. slow cooker, combine the first 5 INGREDIENTS; top with pork chops. Cover and cook on low until meat is tender, 3-4 hours.

2. Remove meat to a serving platter; keep warm. Skim fat from cooking juices; transfer to a small saucepan. Then bring liquid to a boil. Combine cornstarch and water until smooth. Gradually stir into the pan. Bring to a boil; cook and stir until thickened, about 2 minutes. Serve with meat.

33. Goat Cheese & Ham Omelet

Total Time Prep/Total Time: 20 min. Makes 1 serving

INGREDIENTS

- 4 huge egg whites
- 2 teaspoons water
- 1/8 teaspoon pepper
- 1 cut shop ham, finely chopped
- 2 tablespoons finely chopped green pepper
- 2 tablespoons finely chopped onion
- 2 tablespoons disintegrated goat cheddar
- Minced new parsley, optional

DIRECTIONS

1. In a small bowl, whisk egg whites, water and pepper until mixed; mix in ham, green pepper and onion. Heat a huge nonstick skillet covered with cooking splash over medium-high heat. Pour in egg white combination. Blend should set quickly at edges. As egg whites set, push cooked segments toward the middle, allowing uncooked egg to stream under.

2. At the point when no fluid egg remains, sprinkle goat cheddar on 1 side. Overlap omelet fifty-fifty; slide onto a plate. Whenever wanted, sprinkle with parsley.

34. Orange-Glazed Pork with Sweet Potatoes

Total Time Prep: 20 min. Bake: 55 min. + standing

Makes 6 servings

INGREDIENTS

- 1 pound yams (around 2 medium)
- 2 medium apples
- 1 medium orange
- 1 teaspoon salt
- 1/2 teaspoon pepper
- 1 cup squeezed orange
- 2 tablespoons brown sugar
- 2 teaspoons cornstarch
- 1 teaspoon ground cinnamon
- 1 teaspoon ground ginger
- 2 pork tenderloins (around 1 pound each)

DIRECTIONS

1. Preheat oven to 350°. Strip yams; center apples. Cut potatoes, apples and orange transversely into 1/4-in. - thick cuts. Organize in a foil-lined 15x10x1-in. heating container covered with cooking shower; sprinkle with salt and pepper. Cook 10 minutes.

2. Then, in a microwave-safe bowl, blend squeezed orange, brown sugar, cornstarch, cinnamon and ginger. Microwave, covered, on high, mixing like clockwork until thickened, 1-2 minutes. Mix until smooth.

3. Spot pork over yam combination; sprinkle with squeezed orange blend. Broil until a thermometer embedded in pork peruses 145° and yams and apples are delicate, 45-55 minutes longer. Eliminate from oven; tent with foil. Let stand 10 minutes prior to cutting.

35. Salmon Veggie Packets

Total Time Prep/Total Time: 30 min. Makes 4 servings

INGREDIENTS

- 2 tablespoons white wine
- 1 tablespoon olive oil
- 1/4 teaspoon salt
- 1/4 teaspoon pepper
- 2 medium sweet yellow peppers, julienned
- 2 cups new sugar snap peas, managed
- SALMON:
- 2 tablespoons white wine
- 1 tablespoon olive oil
- 1 tablespoon ground lemon zing
- 1/2 teaspoon salt

- 1/4 teaspoon pepper
- 4 salmon filets (6 ounces each)
- 1 medium lemon, split

DIRECTIONS

1. Preheat oven to 400°. Cut four 18x15-in. bits of material paper or uncompromising foil: overlay each transversely down the middle, shaping a wrinkle. In a huge bowl, blend wine, oil, salt and pepper. Add vegetables and throw to cover.

2. In a small bowl, blend the initial five salmon INGREDIENTS. To collect, expose one piece of material paper; place a salmon filet on one side. Sprinkle with 2 teaspoons wine combination; top with one-fourth of the vegetables.

3. Overlay paper over fish and vegetables; overlap the open closures multiple times to seal. Rehash with outstanding parcels. Spot on heating sheets.

4. Heat until fish simply starts to chip effectively with a fork, 12-16 minutes, and opening parcels cautiously to allow steam to get away.

5. To serve, press lemon juice over vegetables.

36. Easy protein Lamb meal

Prep Time 15 mins Cook Time 30 mins Total Time 45 mins

INGREDIENTS

- 2 ½ pounds lamb shoulder chops, see note below
- 1 large sweet potato
- 8 red new potatoes
- 2 Tablespoons olive oil
- 2 Tablespoons chopped fresh rosemary
- 1 Tablespoon chopped fresh thyme leaves
- Salt and freshly ground pepper
- 2 large garlic cloves, sliced
- 1 pint grape or cherry tomatoes

- 8 ounces frozen green peas

DIRECTIONS:
1. Preheat oven to 400ºF.
2. Trim the enormous bits of fat from the sheep and cut into 2-inch lumps.
3. Strip the yam and the new potatoes and cut into 2-inch lumps.
4. On an enormous rimmed sheet dish (12x17), throw the sheep and the potatoes with the olive oil, at that point sprinkle the spices overall and throw until equitably covered.
5. Add salt and pepper as you would prefer and throw. (At the point when I make this for my more distant family I leave it off by and large and let everybody add their own. My significant other loves salt and pepper, so when it's simply us, I use it liberally.)
6. Spread the meat and vegetables out on the plate equitably and dissipate the cut garlic on top.
7. Slide this into your preheated oven and meal for 20 minutes, throwing part of the way through cooking. Meat ought to be browned.

(We like our sheep cooked medium-well. Assuming you need your meat more uncommon, start the potatoes and add the meat 5 to 10 minutes after the fact.)

8. Add the tomatoes and the peas to the sheet skillet and cook for an extra 10 minutes.

9. The store where I purchase my meat had 2 kinds of shoulder slashes, sharp edge and round bone. You need the hacks with the round bone; they are simpler to work with. Likewise, you can request that your butcher 3D shape the meat for you to save time at home.

10. In the event that you don't care for sheep, have a go at subbing sirloin steak. You may require less, in light of the fact that sirloin is less greasy than sheep

37. High protein Wonton Soup

Prep Time: 1 HOUR Cook Time: 5 MINUTES Total Time: 1 HOUR 5 MINUTES Servings: 8 servings

INGREDIENTS

- 1 pack wonton coverings (80 coverings)
- Filling
- 1/2 lbs. (230 g) ground lean pork
- 1/2 lbs. (230 g) stripped shrimp, chopped into little pieces
- 1 tablespoon finely minced ginger
- 2 green onions , finely chopped
- 1 tablespoon light soy sauce (or soy sauce)
- 2 tablespoons Shaoxing wine (or dry sherry)
- 1/2 teaspoon salt
- 2 tablespoons sesame oil

- (Alternative 1) Chicken soup base
- 8 cups chicken stock
- 8 teaspoons light soy sauce (or soy sauce)
- 8 teaspoons minced ginger
- 8 teaspoons sesame oil
- Salt , to taste
- (Choice 2) Chinese road style soup base
- 8 cups hot stock from the wonton bubbling water
- 8 tablespoons papery dried shrimp , or to taste
- 8 major bits of dried ocean growth for soup , arranged by guidance (*Footnote 1)
- 4 teaspoons chicken bouillon
- 8 teaspoons light soy sauce , or to taste
- 8 teaspoons sesame oil
- Garnishes
- 4 green onions , chopped
- 4 stalks infant bok choy , slice to reduced down (or 4 cups infant spinach)
- 1 bunch cilantro, chopped (Optional)
- Hand crafted stew oil , to taste (Optional)

DIRECTIONS

1. Make the filling

2. Without a food processor: Combine ground pork, shrimp, ginger, green onion, soy sauce, Shaoxing wine, salt and sesame oil in a major bowl. Blend well in with a fork until everything consolidates well together and the combination feels somewhat tacky.

3. With a food processor or a blender: coarsely cleave the ginger and green onion. Add all the filling INGREDIENTS with the exception of the shrimp. Blend until it frames a velvety paste. Add the shrimp and mix once more, until the shrimp are finely chopped however don't turn into a paste.

4. Wrap the wonton

5. To make wontons, place a wonton covering in one hand, scoop a teaspoon of wonton filling and spot it close to the restricted side of the wonton covering (you can add more filling to the wonton on the off chance that you like, as long as you can in any case wrap it). Overlap the restricted side over the filling; at that point roll the filling right through the opposite side of the covering. Tie the two finishes and press

together to bolt the filling inside the covering. Brush a dainty layer of water onto the wonton covering and press the closures together.

6. Make each wonton in turn, and line up every one of the wontons on a major wooden cutting board. In the event that you're not going to heat up the wontons promptly, utilize a moist paper towel (or cheesecloth) to cover the wontons to keep them from drying out.

7. On the off chance that you're not going to heat up the wontons that very day, place them in a water/air proof holder with a few layers of wet paper towels on the base. Thusly, they can be put away in the cooler for as long as 2 days.

8. (Alternative 1) Make the chicken soup base

9. Consolidate the chicken stock, ginger, and soy sauce in a pot. Heat to the point of boiling. Let bubble for 10 minutes. Go to least heat to keep warm and begin cooking wontons (see beneath).

10. Plan 8 medium-sized dishes. Add the cooked wontons and bok choy. Add 2 tablespoons green onion, 1 tablespoon soy sauce and 1/2 teaspoon sesame oil into each bowl. Pour in 1

and 1/2 cups hot stock. Trimming with cilantro and stew oil, if using.

11. Serve hot.

12. (Alternative 2) Make the road seller style soup base

13. To get ready 1 serving of wonton soup base, add a major spoon of cilantro, 1 tablespoon papery dried shrimps, a liberal piece of dried kelp, 1/4 teaspoon chicken bouillon, and some child bok choy into a major bowl. Rehash the interaction to set up the remainder of the soup base in the other serving bowls. Cook wontons (see beneath).

14. To make 1 serving of wonton soup, utilize a spoon to move cooked wontons, bok choy, and the hot soup into a serving bowl with every one of the INGREDIENTS from the past advance. Sprinkle 1 teaspoon soy sauce and 1 teaspoon sesame oil into the bowl and give it a delicate mix. The soup ought to be golden hued. Add additional soy sauce or salt if the soup isn't sufficiently pungent. Dissipate green onion on top. Enhancement with cilantro and stew oil, if using.

15. Serve hot.

16. Heated up the wonton

17. To heat up the wontons, heat a major pot of water until bubbling. Add 10 to 20 wontons all at once and bubble over medium heat until wontons are drifting on the outside of the water. Keep on bubbling until the coverings are swollen, around 1 to 2 minutes for little wontons and 2 to 3 minutes for greater ones. Take a wonton out with an opened spoon and split it with a chopstick or fork. On the off chance that the wonton is cooked through, stop heat quickly and move the wontons to singular serving bowls. If not, keep on bubbling until cooked through.

18. Whenever you've cooked the wontons, add the bok choy. Let cook until delicate. Eliminate from the pot, channel well, and put in a safe spot.

19. To cook frozen wontons

20. Heat a huge pot of water to the point of boiling over high heat. Add wontons. Mix tenderly to keep from staying. Cook until heating the water to the point of boiling once more. Go to medium-low heat. Cover the pot with a little hole on one side, to forestall spilling. Keep

bubbling for 2 minutes (3 minutes for bigger wontons). Remain adjacent to the pot the entire chance to screen the stock. On the off chance that the stock begins to spill, reveal and mix, and supplant the cover. Uncover and keep cooking for one more moment, or until the wontons are cooked through.

21. There are numerous kinds of dried ocean growth. My unique formula utilized a sort of moment ocean growth that will rehydrate quickly once positioned into the hot soup. There are different kinds of fish that require some splashing prior to using. Peruse the rear of your bundle and adhere to the guidelines as needs be.

22. The sustenance realities for this formula are determined dependent on 1 bowl of chicken-stock based soup containing 10 wontons.

38. Easy Chicken And Shrimp

INGREDIENTS:

- Chicken and shrimp
- 2-tablespoons vegetable oil
- 1-chicken breast, cut into bite-sized pieces
- ¼ cup cornstarch
- 10-medium shrimp, peeled peanut sauce
- ¼ cup of creamy peanut butter
- 2-tablespoons water
- 1-tablespoon sugar
- 1-tablespoon reduced-sodium soy sauce
- 1-teaspoon rice vinegar
- 1-teaspoon lime juice
- ⅛ teaspoon red pepper flakes
- Curry coconut sauce
- 1-teaspoon olive oil

- 1-teaspoon sesame oil
- ⅛ teaspoon red pepper flakes
- 2-cloves garlic, finely chopped
- 1-small onion, chopped
- 1-teaspoon ginger, finely chopped
- ½ cup water
- ½ teaspoon ground cumin
- ½ teaspoon ground coriander
- 1-teaspoon paprika
- ¼ teaspoon salt (or to taste)
- ¼ teaspoon pepper (or to taste)
- ¼ teaspoon allspice
- ¼ teaspoon turmeric
- 1-can (14 ounces) of coconut milk
- 1-medium carrot, cut julienne
- 1-small zucchini, julienned
- ½ cup of frozen peas
- Garnish
- ½ cup coconut flakes, toasted
- ¼ cup peanuts, chopped
- 2-green onions, cut or chopped into julienne
- Sesame seeds (optional)
- 2-cups of rice, cooked

DIRECTIONS:

1. Heat the two tablespoons of oil in a large frying pan. Salt and pepper the chicken pieces to taste and dip them in the cornstarch. Do the same with the shrimp.

2. When the oil is hot, leave the chicken with it and cook until it starts to brown, about a few minutes. Then do the same with the shrimp, cook the shrimp until it just starts to turn pink.

3. Place the chicken and shrimp on a plate and set aside.

4. In a small saucepan, heat all the INGREDIENTS for the peanut sauce. Cook until just starting to boil, then remove from heat and set aside.

5. In another saucepan over medium heat, add 1-teaspoon of vegetable oil, vegetable oil, and ground red pepper flakes. Add the garlic, sliced onion, and ginger and cook until the onion is soft. Add the water and all the spices for the sauce and stir to mix. Bring this mixture to a boil. When it starts to boil, add the coconut milk and bring it back to a boil. Then reduce the heat and simmer for 20 minutes or until the sauce thickens nicely.

6. When the sauce has thickened, add the julienned carrots and zucchini and stir in the peas last—Cook for about 10 minutes more, or until the carrots are tender.

7. Before serving, place some rice on each plate and add some chicken and shrimp. Cover with the sauce and put some of the peanut sauce on top. Garnish with one or more of the above toppings under garnish.

39. Chicken with Broccoli and Sweet Potato Wedges

Prep time: 30 min Serves 4

INGREDIENTS

- 8 (3 1/2-oz.) chicken drumsticks, cleaned 1 tablespoon new lemon juice 1/8 teaspoons kosher salt, isolated 1/2 teaspoon poultry preparing 1 teaspoon garlic powder, separated 1/8 teaspoon newly ground dark pepper 2 huge eggs, gently thumped 1 cup panko (Japanese breadcrumbs) 1/2 ounces Parmesan cheddar, ground (around 1/3 cup) 1 teaspoon dried oregano 1 teaspoon dried parsley pieces (optional) Cooking splash 2 (7-oz.) yams, each cut into 8 wedges 2 tablespoons olive oil, partitioned 1/2 teaspoon paprika 1/2 teaspoon bean stew powder 7 cups broccoli florets (around 12 oz.) 1 garlic clove, squashed or ground 5 lemon wedges

DIRECTIONS:

1. Preheat oven to 425°F.

2. Spot chicken in an enormous bowl. Shower with lemon squeeze, and sprinkle with 3/8 teaspoon salt, poultry preparing, 1/2 teaspoon garlic powder, and dark pepper; throw to join.

3. Spot eggs in a shallow dish. Consolidate panko, Parmesan, oregano, and parsley, if using, in another shallow dish. Plunge every drumstick in eggs at that point dig in panko blend. Spot drumsticks on a rimmed heating sheet covered with cooking shower; dispose of outstanding egg and panko blend. Coat highest points of drumsticks with cooking splash. Prepare at 425°F for 15 minutes.

4. Consolidate potatoes, 1 tablespoon oil, staying 1/2 teaspoon garlic powder, paprika, bean stew powder, and 3/8 teaspoon salt; throw to

cover. Mastermind potatoes on one portion of another rimmed preparing sheet covered with cooking shower. Spot in oven with chicken, and heat at 425°F for 10 minutes.

5. Consolidate broccoli, staying 1 tablespoon oil, garlic clove, and staying 3/8 teaspoon salt. Eliminate heating sheet with potatoes from oven; turn potatoes over, and add broccoli to other portion of container. Spot in oven with chicken, and heat at 425°F for 20 minutes or until chicken and potatoes are finished. Crush 1 lemon wedge over broccoli. Serve remaining lemon wedges with the dinner.

40. Puff Pastry Chicken Bundles

Total Time Prep: 30 min. Bake: 20 min. Makes 8 servings

INGREDIENTS

- 8 boneless skinless chicken breast halves (about 6 ounces each)
- 1 teaspoon salt
- 1/2 teaspoon pepper
- 40 large spinach leaves
- 1 carton (8 ounces) spreadable chive and onion cream cheese
- 1/2 cup chopped walnuts, toasted
- 2 sheets frozen puff pastry, thawed
- 1 large egg
- 1/2 teaspoon cold water

DIRECTIONS

1. Preheat oven to 400°. Cut a longwise cut in every chicken bosom half to inside 1/2 in. of the opposite side; open meat so it lies level. Cover with cling wrap; pound with a meat mallet to 1/8-in. thickness. Eliminate plastic wrap. Sprinkle with salt and pepper.

2. Spot five spinach leaves on every chicken bosom half. Spoon a meager 2 tablespoons of cream cheddar down the focal point of every chicken bosom half; sprinkle with 1 tablespoon pecans. Move up chicken; wrap up closes.

3. Unfurl puff baked good; cut into eight segments. Fold each into a 7-in. square. Spot chicken on one portion of each square; overlay other portion of baked good over chicken. Pleat edges with fork. Consolidate egg and cold water; brush over edges of cake.

4. Heat on a lubed 15x10x1-in. heating sheet until a thermometer peruses 165°, 20-25 minutes.

41. 4 Easy Green Pepper Steak

Total Time Prep/Total Time: 30 min. Makes 4 servings

INGREDIENTS

- 1 tablespoon cornstarch
- 1/4 cup reduced-sodium soy sauce
- 1/4 cup water
- 2 tablespoons canola oil, divided
- 1 pound beef top sirloin steak, cut into 1/4-in.-thick strips
- 2 small onions, cut into thin wedges
- 2 celery ribs, sliced diagonally
- 1 medium green pepper, cut into 1-inch pieces
- 2 medium tomatoes, cut into wedges
- Hot cooked rice

DIRECTIONS

1. Combine cornstarch, soy sauce and water until smooth. In a large skillet, heat 1 tablespoon oil over medium-high heat; stir-fry beef until browned, 2-3 minutes. Remove from pan.

2. Stir-fry onions, celery and pepper in remaining oil 3 minutes. Stir cornstarch mixture; add to pan. Bring to a boil; cook and stir until thickened and bubbly, 1-2 minutes. Stir in tomatoes and beef; heat through. Present with rice.

42. Healthy Seafood Soup

22 MINUTES MIN 2 BOWLS SERVINGS

INGREDIENTS

- 2½ C vegetable stock
- 4 ocean scallops, washed and wiped off
- 2 C gluten free noodles, cooked as coordinated
- 1 carrot, stripped and julienned
- 2 celery ribs, meagerly cut
- 2 red radish, managed and daintily cut
- 1 C spring peas, shelled, pods disposed of
- 2 C shiitake mushroom covers, daintily cut
- 1 scallion, managed and daintily cut
- 2 cloves garlic, shredded
- 1 T new ginger, cleaned and shredded
- 1 T unsalted spread
- 1 T additional virgin olive oil

- 1 tsp. fit salt, more to taste
- run sriracha or other hot sauce
- embellish with sprinkling of miniature greens

DIRECTIONS

1. Wash and afterward strip, trim, cut hack, cut, dice or julienne vegetables as you wish. Wash ocean scallops and afterward wipe off.

2. Empty vegetable stock into a medium-sized pot. Heat to the point of boiling and afterward decrease to stew. Mix in garlic, ginger and salt. Cover.

3. Heat 5 cups of salted water to the point of boiling. Add dried noodles and cook as coordinated. Channel and gap into two soup bowls.

4. Simultaneously, carry a medium measured skillet to medium-high temperature. Add spread and olive oil, permitting them to mix and come to temperature. Add scallops, being mindful so as not to swarm them in the skillet. Burn one side, around 3-4 minutes, turn over and rehash. When cooked, eliminate from skillet and permit to rest.

5. Return stock to a bubble. Add vegetables and cook for 4 minutes.

6. Using an opened spoon, eliminate the entirety of the vegetables from the stock. Spoon onto cooked noodles, partitioning them uniformly between the two dishes.

7. Move two singed scallops into each bowl. Spoon equivalent measures of bubbling stock into each bowl.

8. Add a scramble of hot sauce to each bowl and trimming both with a sprinkling of micro-greens.

43.   Beef Lettuce Cups with Carrot & Daikon Slaw

SERVINGS 4 PREP TIME 40 min COOK TIME 5 min

DURATION 45 min

INGREDIENTS

- 1/4 cup rice vinegar
- 1 tbsp. plus 1/2 tsp. raw honey, divided
- 1/8 tsp. sea salt
- 1 carrot, peeled and cut into matchsticks (1/ cup)
- 1 daikon radish, cut into matchsticks (1/cup) (TIP: If you can't find daikon radish, regular radish works well here too.)
- 1 tsp. sesame oil
- 10 oz. lean ground beef

- 1/2 cup finely chopped red onion
- 3 cloves garlic, minced
- 1 tbsp. peeled and minced fresh ginger
- 1 1/3 cups BPA-free canned unsalted black beans, drained and rinsed
- 1 tbsp. reduced-sodium soy sauce
- 12 romaine lettuce leaves
- 2 tbsp. chopped roasted unsalted peanuts
- 2 tbsp. thinly sliced scallions

DIRECTIONS

1. Firstly In a medium bowl, whisk together vinegar, 1 tbsp. honey and salt. Add carrot and radish; toss to coat. Cover and transfer to refrigerator to marinate until tender and chilled, at least 2 hours or overnight.

2. Heat a large nonstick skillet on medium and brush with oil. Then Add beef and sauté until no longer pink, about 5 minutes. Push beef to one side of skillet. To other side, add onion, garlic and ginger; sauté until onion softens, about 2 minutes.

3. Add beans, soy sauce and remaining 1/2 tsp. honey and stir all INGREDIENTS together; simmer for 3 minutes, stirring occasionally.

4. Drain liquid from slaw. Fill in each lettuce leaf with 1/4 cup beef-bean mixture; top it with slaw. Garnish with peanuts and scallions.

44. Chicken enchilada bowl

Prep Time: 20 minutes Cook Time: 30 minutes Total Time: 50 minutes Yield: 4 servings

INGREDIENTS

- 2 tablespoons coconut oil (for singing chicken)
- 1 pound of boneless, skinless chicken thighs
- 3/4 cup red enchilada sauce (formula from Low Carb Maven)
- 1/4 cup water
- 1/4 cup chopped onion
- 1-4 oz. can diced green chilies
- Fixings (don't hesitate to modify)
- 1 entire avocado, diced
- 1 cup shredded cheddar (I utilized gentle cheddar)
- 1/4 cup chopped cured jalapenos
- 1/2 cup sharp cream

- 1 roma tomato, chopped
- Optional: serve over plain cauliflower rice (or Mexican cauliflower rice) for a more complete supper!

DIRECTIONS

1. In a pot or Dutch oven over medium heat liquefy the coconut oil. When hot, burn chicken thighs until gently brown.

2. Pour in enchilada sauce and water at that point adds onion and green chilies. Decrease heat to a stew and cover. Cook chicken for 17-25 minutes or until chicken is delicate and completely cooked through to in any event 165 degrees inner temperature.

3. Carefully eliminate the chicken and spot onto a work surface. Hack or shred chicken (your inclination) at that point add it back into the pot. Let the chicken stew uncovered for an extra 10 minutes to ingest enhance and permit the sauce to decrease a bit.

4. To Serve, top with avocado, cheddar, jalapeno, sharp cream, tomato, and some other wanted garnishes. Don't hesitate to redo these to your

inclination. Serve alone or over cauliflower rice whenever wanted simply make certain to refresh your own nourishment data depending on the situation.

Conclusion

I would like to thank you all for going through this book. All the recipes in this book are healthy meal recipes which are much beneficial. All recipes are very easy to maintain a healthy life schedule. Try these dishes at home and appreciate.

Wish you good luck!

CPSIA information can be obtained
at www.ICGtesting.com
Printed in the USA
BVHW051659120521
607132BV00002B/92